Lincolnshire Echo

Lincoln

Moments in Time

Lincolnshire Echo

Lincoln
Moments in Time

compiled by Peter Washbourn

The Breedon Books
Publishing Company
Derby

First published in Great Britain by

The Breedon Books Publishing Company Limited

Breedon House, Unit 3, Parker Centre, Derby DE21 4SZ.

2000

ISBN 1 85983 208 3

Printed and bound by Butler & Tanner Ltd., Selwood Printing Works, Caxton Road,

Frome, Somerset.

Colour separations and jacket printing by GreenShires Group Ltd, Leicester.

Contents

Introduction

WHAT is a moment?

The dictionary lists it as a short indefinite period of time, or a specific instant or point in time.

So *Moments in Time* is a selection of some of these short periods or specific points as they were captured by *Lincolnshire Echo* photographers.

One of the problems in compiling a book of this nature is what to include and what to leave out.

When I compiled *Memory Lane Lincoln and Lincolnshire* last year, I tried to include something from all of the decades of the century up to the Seventies.

This time, I have started at 1930 and ended at the Silver Jubilee celebrations of 1977.

The *Lincolnshire Echo's* archives of negatives, which have been used exclusively in this volume, start in 1930 and for the next 40 years, are mostly on glass plates.

In order to put this collection into some sort of order, I have made four 'chapters' devoted to each decade, Thirties, Forties, Fifties and Sixties.

Added to this are sections of Lincoln scenes and changes in scene. One section concerns the visit of stars of the entertainment world to the city, another to the activities of youth and there is also a section dealing with celebration in Lincoln, two Coronations and two Silver Jubilees.

As well as selecting pictures which show the changes in Lincoln, I have also assembled photographs of some of the events, which I hope will bring back happy memories to those who remember them and in some instances, appear in the pictures.

Once again, I must thank Russell Kirk, the photographic printer at the *Echo*, for his help and patience and also the numerous people who have provided me with information for some of the captions. And of course, it would not have been possible without the skills of the numerous photographers employed by the *Lincolnshire Echo* over the past 70 years.

Also, a very big thank you to my wife Patricia, who has typed all the captions from my rather untidy handwriting and also checked the proofs with me.

Producing this book has brought back many memories and reminded me of some of the events I attended and photographed since becoming an *Echo* photographer in 1960.

Peter Washbourn
Summer, 2000

The Thirties

IT WAS not until this decade that the *Lincolnshire Echo* employed a staff photographer and we start this journey through *Moments in Time* with a look at some of the pictures taken in that decade.

Some of the scenes will still be familiar today, but many show buildings which have now disappeared and been replaced. In some instances these replacements too have vanished.

Most of the pictures retained in the *Lincolnshire Echo* archives from this period show scenes, rather than pictures of people and a search through copies of the *Echo* indicates that this type of picture was most common.

The Thirties was a time when there was much change in Lincoln. Extensions to the Lincoln County Hospital were being built and there were several changes to the roads in the city to make improvements for the increasing motor traffic, including the introduction of the city's first set of automatic traffic signals and pedestrian crossings.

It also saw the demolition of St Peter at Arches Church in the city centre and the adjacent Butter Market was closed and replaced with a new Central Market in Sincil Street.

There are some pictures which look as if they could have been taken in a Lincolnshire village. Only close scrutiny shows them to be within the city boundary.

Big events of the decade were the Silver Jubilee of King George V and the Coronation of King George VI. These events have been dealt with in the section on celebrations.

McDakin's Bridge connected Boultham Avenue with Coulson Road and was erected by the Ellison family, who lived at Boultham Hall. When this picture was taken in the Thirties, horse-drawn wagons were still in use. (RI-21)

It looks like a village scene, but this was Langworthgate in 1935, with a dairy on the right. (RI-127)

In the Thirties, Gordon Road, linking Bailgate with St Paul's Lane, was a hotchpotch of buildings – eventually to be replaced by new shops. (RI-81)

It might be difficult to decide where this cottage was in 1934, but it stood behind the newly-opened Lincoln Technical College. The buildings in the background are located on Lindum Road, at the foot of Greestone Stairs. (RI-119)

The caretakers' cottage, at the back of the Usher Art Gallery, as it was in 1937. (RI-180)

Harrisons shop, at the corner of Melville Street and Waterside South, in the Thirties, sold radios or wireless sets (as they were called), and boxes of these are lined up on the pavement, the price being £14 14s, quite a considerable amount of money in those days. Harrisons were also tobacconists and Magpies Square Post Office was in the same building. (RI-124)

A procession of mayors and mace bearers arrive at the Usher Art Gallery, in May 1937. At the time, an exhibition was being staged at the gallery to mark the Coronation of King George VI. (RI-774)

Lincoln's old gas works, on Carholme Road, Lincoln, was known as the Newland Works, where the city's gas supply was made until the Bracebridge works opened in 1876. These buildings were demolished in 1933. (RI-95)

The gas distribution centre on the corner of Carholme Road and Brayford Wharf, which also served as a showroom. (RI-93)

Inside the gas distribution centre, shelves are piled with meters, spares and gas lamps. (RI-93)

It's hard to believe that this scene is right in the heart of Lincoln, in Swanpool Court, just off the High Street opposite the Cornhill. It was taken in 1933. (RI-18)

Lincoln's new Technical College, on Cathedral Street, which opened in 1932. (RI-16)

The heat engine laboratory at the new Technical College. (RI-16)

In 1934, this was the St George's Mission Church in Doddington Road. A new church was built in 1960, at the corner of Doddington Road and Eastbrook Road. (RI-91)

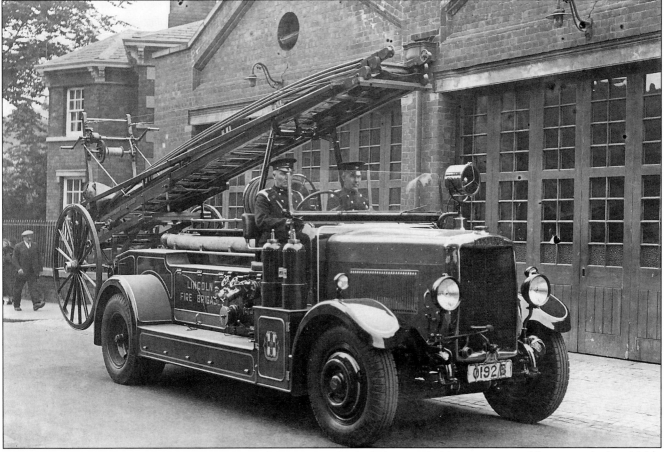

Lincoln had a new fire engine in 1936 equipped with pump and wheeled escape ladder. It is pictured here outside the old fire station on Monks Road. (RI-718)

The Whit Monday walk, in 1935, travels up High Street, with a procession of Sunday School Queens and banners. (RI-521)

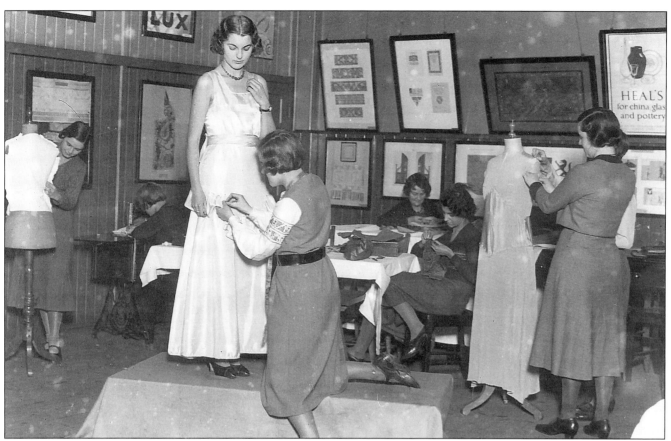

A dressmaking demonstration in 1932, at the City School, Lincoln in the Art Room. (RI-546)

The world's smallest working car, in 1936, took part in a carnival parade to raise funds for Lincoln County Hospital. (RI-577)

Lincoln County Hospital parade in 1936 had a carnival queen and many people in fancy dress. This picture was taken in Broadgate, at its junction with St Rumbold Street and it was reported in the *Echo* that 8,000 people were in Broadgate to see the parade. (RI-577)

A peaceful scene around the ornamental pond at the West Common, in 1932. (RI-87)

The footbridge at Stamp End Lock in 1935, and in the background, the now vanished houses and Brickmakers' Arms public house. (RI-132)

Extension work under way at Lincoln County Hospital. (RI-53)

Extensions to this part of Lincoln County Hospital were almost complete in September 1931 when this picture was taken. (RI-53)

Museum of the past. Greyfriars was the home of the City and County Museum for almost 90 years before being closed to make a temporary home for Lincoln Central Library. This picture shows the layout during the Thirties. (RI-42)

Were they playing ice hockey on the frozen Brayford, in 1935? Looking at the skaters, they all appear to have a stick in their hands. (RI-522)

Some looked confident, some not so, when they took to the ice on the frozen lake at Hartsholme Park, just two days before Christmas in 1935. (RI-522)

Repairs to Lincoln Stonebow in 1930, but what would the Health and Safety Executive make of that scaffolding today? (RI-45)

This wintry scene in Lincoln Arboretum could have been taken anytime – it was sometime in the Thirties. (RI-81)

The ovens at Whitton's Bakery come in handy for roasting the joints of beef for the annual Robin Dinner, for youngsters, in January 1933. (RI-549)

The water level of Brayford Pool was lowered considerably in 1932 when the pool was dredged to remove years of mud and silt. (RI-109)

Dredgers at work in 1932 clearing the channels of Brayford Pool. (RI-109)

Lincoln Horse Fair had only moved to the West Common from the High Street, a few years earlier, when this picture was taken in 1934. (RI-473)

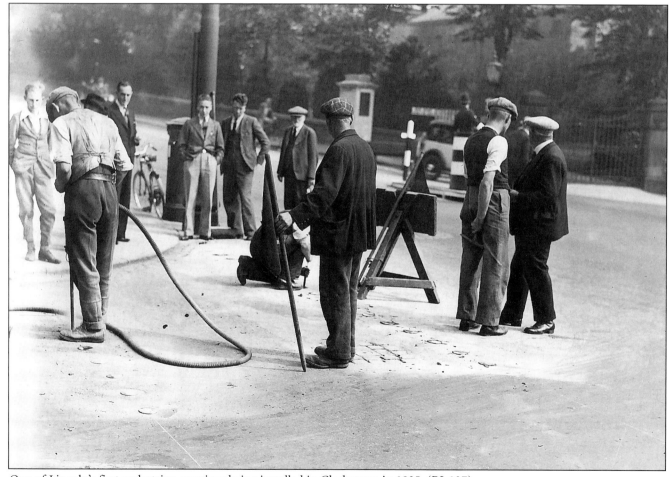

One of Lincoln's first pedestrian crossings being installed in Clasketgate in 1935. (RI-137)

St Benedict's Church during restoration work in 1932. (RI-39)

Lincoln's first Belisha crossing was installed in 1935, on Newland, near to the junction with Lucy Tower Street. (RI-137)

When this picture was taken in the Thirties, only fragments were left of the mansion known as 'John o' Gaunt's Palace', in Lincoln High Street. (RI-13)

This 15-16th century building, at the junction of Steep Hill and Michaelgate, was still the Harlequin Inn in the early Thirties, before being converted into antique and book shops. (RI-8)

This Thirties picture of Lindum Road and Cathedral Street is full of nostalgia. A garage, religious meeting hall, offices and a boarding house have now all been replaced by accommodation for college students. Down Cathedral Street can be seen the buildings of the City School, now replaced by college buildings. (RI-76)

Monks Manor, home of the Ruston family, stood just off the Greetwell Road. It was demolished in the early Thirties – an architectural loss to the city. (RI-75)

Monks Manor, being demolished in the Thirties. (RI-102)

The Lincoln Board of Guardians met for the last time in March 1930 and posed for this photograph. Formed to administer the Poor Law, they handed the work over to the Public Assistance Committee. (RI-1238)

Lincoln's Butter Market had to be shored up in 1934, after the demolition of the adjacent St Peter at Arches Church. The market itself was removed a few years later. (RI-46)

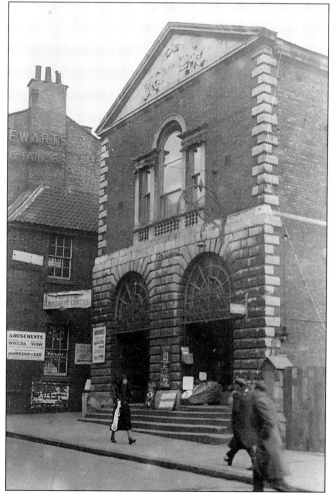

The front of Lincoln Butter Market in the Thirties before it was removed and rebuilt into the new market hall in Sincil Street. (RI-46)

What a wonderful picture of the interior of Lincoln Butter Market in the mid Thirties, with the 'country ladies' selling their home-made produce. (RI-177)

The new Central Market under construction in 1938. (RI-194)

Ready for the opening, Lincoln Central Market, which replaced the old butter market at St Peter at Arches, had a section which could be locked off from the stalls and at one time, wrestling matches were held in it. (RI-194)

Building sun-shelters in the grounds of the Usher Art Gallery in the early Thirties, shortly after the building had been opened. (RI-64)

At the 'country' end of Nettleham Road, a new roundabout was constructed at the junction with Longdales Road and Ruskin Avenue. (RI-149)

Improvements to the road layout were made in Northgate in 1938, at the city end of Nettleham Road. (RI-192)

It was in the Thirties that Lincoln received its first set of traffic lights and these were installed at the junction of West Parade and The Avenue. (RI-27)

Monks Road, near the Arboretum, during major resurfacing work in 1938. (RI-189)

Thornbridge was very narrow when this picture was taken in 1935. During the course of the next few years, the bridge was replaced and the road widened to take an increasing flow of traffic. Looking west, the old houses on Waterside South, on the left, were to be demolished, to make way for the Thornbridge Hotel. (RI-169)

The Bowling Green public house on Wragby Road, in 1934, with a *Lincolnshire Echo* delivery van in its car park. (RI-22)

A busy High Street scene in 1934 when traffic was much lighter than before the area was pedestrianised in the Seventies. Many of the business names have gone today, although most of the buildings remain, some with a facelift. (RI-103)

Castle Hill, in the early Thirties before the houses of the left were demolished. In World War Two, the area was used as an emergency water reservoir and is now a car park. (RI-2)

In the late Thirties, Pottergate Arch, was closed to traffic with the building of the new road, to the right on this picture. Repairs were also carried out on the arch which formed part of the Close Wall in Lincoln. (RI-222)

The Lincoln Scene

Steep Hill, Lincoln, in January 1935 and what a picture of nostalgia it presents. A delivery boy, with a tradesman's bike and window cleaners busy at their work. A few shoppers trudge up the hill. Today, the scene would most likely show tourists. (RI-58)

THIS section of the *Moments in Time* is guaranteed to bring back many memories, although in some instances, you can go out today and see the scenes pictured with hardly any change.

Only a few of the photographs depict buildings which are no longer around. Others are of buildings as they were half a century ago; they are still there today, after a facelift and not always for the better.

Do you remember the days when the lamplighter made his rounds, to check the gas mantle and rewind the clock? Or the 'old' Ropewalk, with railway sidings on each side?

Memories of 'Big Wesley', 'Bainbridges' bridge, Mawer and Collingham's department store and 'Binks for Bikes' are just some of the scenes pictured in this section.

This picture of Steep Hill was taken in 1961. Today, very little has changed, only new housing at Neustadt Court, on the empty land at the bottom right corner. (RI-3418)

Looking down Danesgate in the Thirties, the back of Wesley Methodist Chapel rises over the rooftops with the spire of St Swithins's Church in the picture. (RI-210)

This was the servicing department, in Scorer Street, for West's (Lincoln) Ltd, whose showrooms were in High Street. The picture was taken in 1931 and West's left them nearly 50 years later. Now they are used by City Tyre Experts. (RI-26)

The view over Brayford Pool in 1937. Hovis' Mill is clearly visible on the left and all of the properties on Brayford Wharf North are 'in business'. (RI-182)

There were still some gas lamps left in 1962 for the gaslighter to attend, including this one in James Street, Lincoln. (RI-1434)

Ye Olde Crowne, in Clasketgate, picture in 1937, was built in 'Mock Tudor' style. In the Sixties, some of the scenes of the film *The Wild and The Willing* were shot in its interior. (RI-186)

A scene in 1955 which is completely different today. The Ropewalk, Lincoln runs through the middle of 'railway land', the Holmes Yard being on the left and the old Midland Yard on the right. Today the former is the site of the University of Lincolnshire and Humberside, the latter, a shopping centre. (RI-850)

The back of the old Harlequin Inn, dating from the 15/16th centuries, parts of the building being below road surface. It has been called 'The Crooked House' and even 'The Bendy House'. This misty day picture was taken in 1935. (RI-17)

The Wesleyan Methodist Chapel or 'Big Wesley' as it was better known was built in 1836 and demolished in 1963. During World War Two, basement rooms were used as an annexe by The City School. (RI-479)

'Big Wesley' was still in use in 1959 when these road improvements in Clasketgate were under way. The spire is on St Hugh's Roman Catholic Church, in Monks Road. (RI-3620)

Mawer and Collingham's shop in High Street was a business founded in 1820, by William Mawer and his son-in-law Joseph Collingham. In 1876, it became the first shop in Lincoln to give its staff a half-day's holiday on Saturdays. In 1980, it was taken over by the House of Fraser Group and was re-named Binns.

The old Whitefriar's House, in Akrills's Passage, was much more visible in 1955 than it is today. (RI-1027)

St Paul's Church, in Westgate had only a few years to go in 1967, before it was demolished in the early Seventies. It was the last of a long line of churches built on the site which possibly saw Lincoln's first Christian church. (RI-999)

The Children's Home, in 1935 was located in Saxon Street in this very imposing stone building. Just look at the number of chimney pots. There must be one for every room in the house. (RI-130)

Bracebridge Hall was built in the 1880s and was the home of Francis J. Clarke. This picture was taken in 1931. Today, the hall, now known as Grosvenor Hall, is a private nursing home for the elderly. (RI-77)

Looking more like a village scene rather than in Lincoln this view of St Botolph's Church is from St Botolph's Crescent. (RI-3838)

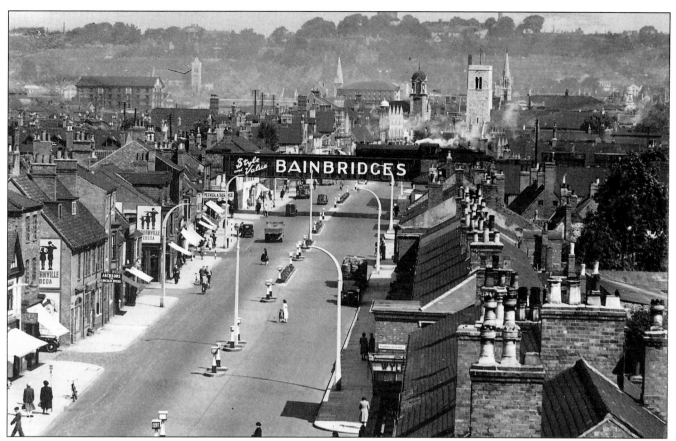

There was little traffic about in 1950 when this picture was taken from St Botolph's Church tower. The bridge carrying the railway avoiding line over High Street, carries an advertisement for Bainbridges department store. (RI-662)

It was very cold in February 1936 and an ice-breaker was needed to keep a channel open for the barges on the Brayford Pool. (RI-67)

W. J. Binks & Co had their motor and cycle showroom in St Benedict Square from 1895 until the Sixties. This picture, taken in 1932, shows the business before it's name was changed to Binks (Cycles) Ltd. (RI-25)

When this photograph was taken in the early Thirties, traffic travelling up Pottergate went to the left of the arch and that moving downhill went through it. The wall on the right was later removed and a new road built. (RI-6)

In 1959, the Welcome Café was about to become the East Midlands Electricity Board's showrooms. The building, dating from the 19th century, was designed by Lincoln architect, William Watkins and was originally Peacock Willson's bank. (RI-3853)

Bailgate today looks little changed from this picture taken in 1939. The garage on the right is now used by the White Hart Hotel and the business on the corner of Exchequergate, once a café, is now the Magna Carta public house. (RI-159)

A wintry scene in Castle Hill, in the early Forties when deliveries were still being made by horse-drawn vans. (RI-241)

Bunting hung across Lincoln High Street for the Coronation of King George VI in 1937. This scene, just north of the old Midland Station, shows Sibthorpe House, on the right, with an *Echo* van outside Boots shop. (RI-178)

Rasen Lane Methodist Church pictured in 1957. It was built in 1863, on the site of an earlier chapel of 1849 and was one of two Primitive Methodist Chapels in Lincoln, the other being Portland Place, near the Great Northern Railway Station. (RI-3727)

The gates of Boultham Park came from Monks Manor when that property was demolished in the Thirties. (RI-54)

Thirty years on and the gates have survived the war and are still there today. In this picture taken the spring of 1960, the gardeners at Boultham Park are busy tidying the floral displays. (RI-3684)

Much of the property around Brayford Pool was still in use when this picture was taken in 1954. It was to be almost 20 years before Brayford Head Bridge was replaced by a modern road bridge. (RI-2026)

Woolworths shop frontage in the High Street was a familiar sight in Lincoln for more than 50 years until it was demolished in the late 1980s to make way for the Waterside Centre. Adjoining shops in 1955 were Home and Colonial (grocers), Mac Fisheries and Lipton's (grocers), names which have now gone from the city. (RI-1393)

Newport Arch was still attached to the Lincoln Co-operative Society shop in the early Thirties when this picture was taken. In 1924, the arch received Historic Building status.

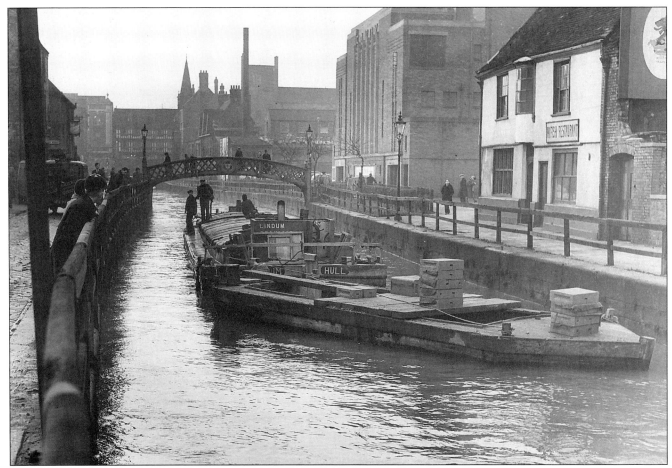

A timeless scene in the Fifties of barges along the River Witham. The cinema was still called the Savoy.

A scene which has remained almost unchanged for 150 years. In 1958, the Victorian prison at Lincoln Castle was receiving attention from builders. (RI-2792)

The Forties

THIS was a time dominated by the events of World War Two and as many pictures from this era were dealt with in Memory Lane, Lincoln and Lincolnshire, they have not been repeated in this book. However, there are a few images reminding us of these dark years but unfortunately, not many negatives from this period survive in the *Lincolnshire Echo* archives.

Those which are included give us some unusual pictures; the Navy marching through Lincoln to support the Army; trial growing of sugarbeet in a Lincoln park and the removal of iron railings and tramlines for scrap metal.

There is also a reminder that horses were still used for corporation duties around the city and that the Duke of Edinburgh visited Lincoln, nine years before the Queen came to open Pelham Bridge.

Workers look on as a Matilda tank rolls out from the Ruston and Hornsby factory in the early Forties. The first Matilda sent to the Middle East was made in Lincoln and before production of these tanks was halted, 400 were made in Lincoln for the British and Russian forces. (RI-740)

Workmen removing the panels of glass from the windows of Lincoln Cathedral, at the start of World War Two, as a precaution against air raids. (RI-225)

Panels from the windows of Lincoln Cathedral being removed for safety. (RI-238)

An undated photograph of a military parade in Lincoln, but probably taken in the Forties, as an anti-tank gun section of the Army travel up Lindum Road. (RI-901)

It's rare to see the Navy in Lincoln, but in 1944, a detachment of sailors marched down Lincoln High Street as part of Salute the Soldier Week. (RI-1294)

There was a queue in 1940 for the exchange of Bread Units, at the Lincoln Food Office. (RI-257)

Hoeing sugarbeet, but in Lincoln? Trials were held in Boultham Park to grow a crop, at a time when import of cane sugar was affected by the war. In the background of this picture, taken in 1940, is Boultham Hall. (RI-234)

The Good Friday procession, in 1941, climbs up Michaelgate, led by the Bishop of Lincoln, the Rt Revd Nugent Hicks. (RI-719)

The United Methodist Chapel, i Silver Street, opened in 1864. When this photograph was taken in 1940, the chapel was about to close and it became warehouse and later a store for the Lincoln Co-operati Society. (RI-105)

The organ in the Methodist Chapel in Silver Street was removed when the chapel closed in 1940 and rebuilt into the new Holy Cross Church. (RI-105)

Holy Cross Church, Skellingthorpe Road, in the final stages of construction in 1940. (RI-237)

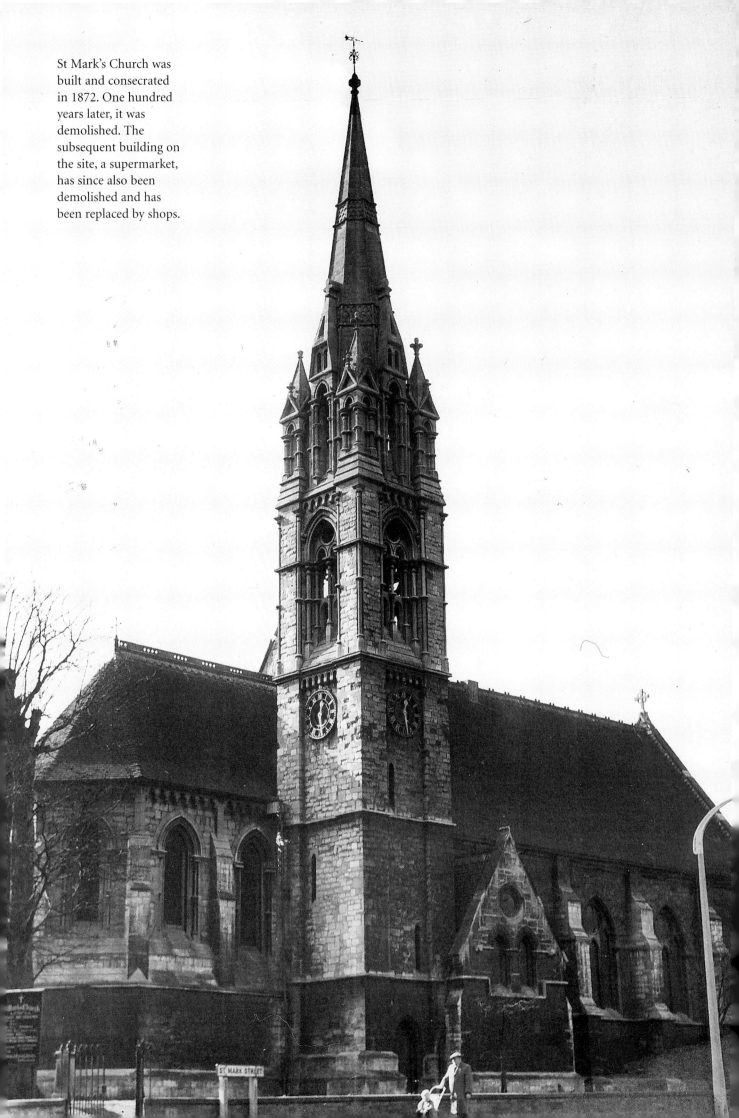

St Mark's Church was built and consecrated in 1872. One hundred years later, it was demolished. The subsequent building on the site, a supermarket, has since also been demolished and has been replaced by shops.

The Saracen's Head Hotel, in Lincoln High Street was one of the oldest hostelries in Lincoln, with records of its licence dating back several centuries. It closed in 1959, although these photographs were taken some 20-30 years earlier. During World War Two, it was a popular place with aircrews, who named it the 'Snake Pit'. (RI-834)

The interior of the Saracen's Head Hotel, Lincoln. (RI-834)

Protection on the windows of Battles' shop, north of the Stonebow, date this as a wartime picture, when many windows had similar protection against bomb blast. Battles' shop survived – their warehouse in Saltergate fell victim to a bomb and was destroyed. (RI-233)

Although Lincoln said goodbye to trams in 1929 and the old tracks covered over, the rails were dug up in the summer of 1940 and the metal used for war effort. This scene is at the bottom of Cross o' Cliff Hill. (RI-526)

Many houses had railings in front of them, but they were all cut off and used as scrap metal for the war effort in 1942. This picture was taken on Monks Road. (RI-256)

These buildings on Brayford Wharf East have gone today, being replaced by office blocks and when this picture was taken, *c*.1940, there appears to be some work being done on the footbridge to the railway sheds. (RI-140)

The railings around the exercise yard at the old prison in Lincoln Castle grounds fell victim to the war in 1940, when they were removed for scrap. (RI-226)

Lincolnshire Regiment Trumpeters sound a fanfare from the roof of Lincoln Guildhall to mark the start of Thanksgiving Week, for the end of World War Two in 1945. (RI-520)

There were a lot of interested onlookers in Lincoln High Street, in April 1947, when Arthur Houghton, rode his penny farthing bike through the Stonebow. (RI-264)

A new housing was made in 1949 for the Mote Bell, on Lincoln Guildhall roof. The bell, the oldest such bell in the country, is dated 1371, and rung before every council meeting. (RI-412)

It was 1949 when this picture was taken of Violet, one of the Lincoln Corporation's 'fleet' of horses, used for pulling refuse collection vehicles around the city. (RI-409)

A huge fire destroyed part of the Hovis Mill, on Brayford, in 1947. (RI-798)

One of the firefighters receives attention after breathing in smoke and fumes at the Hovis Mill fire. (RI-798)

Lincoln Horse Fair had been an annual event for many years and until the late Twenties, was held in the High Street. It was moved to the West Common, but in 1947, when this picture was taken, it had only a couple of years to go before it closed. (RI-266)

Repairing the bridge carrying the railway line over the Sincil Drain. An undated picture, but believed to have been taken in the late Forties and early Fifties. (RI-261)

The Duke of Edinburgh came to Lincoln in 1949, to attend a luncheon at the Assembly Rooms as part of a half-a-million pounds appeal for the National Playing Fields Association. Walking along Bailgate, the Duke is accompanied by Lord Heneage and the Mayor of Lincoln Alderman W. H. Martin. (RI-678)

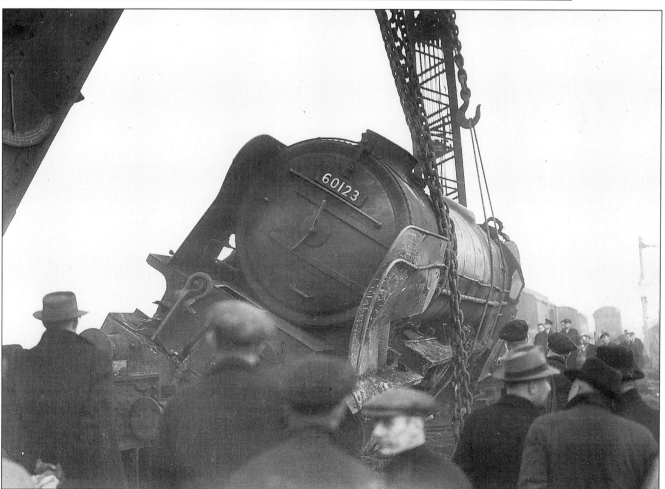

British Railways locomotive 60123 is lifted back on to the tracks, in 1949, after being derailed and rolling down the embankment at Coulson Road. It had collided with a slow moving empty goods train. (RI-619)

Time for a Change

THIS section of *Moments in Time* is bound to evoke memories for many people as the pictures show scenes which have changed, in some cases, beyond recognition.

The houses at the bottom of Steep Hill and Michaelgate were demolished in the late Fifties and have been replaced with modern dwellings.

The building of Pelham Bridge in the same decade meant that much of the Melville Street and Pelham Street area was completely flattened for what was, at that time, Lincoln's most ambitious road scheme.

Changes 20 years earlier saw the removal of St Peter at Arches Church to the new St Giles Estate and the adjacent butter market closed, to be replaced with a new market in Sincil Street. Pictures of this can be found in the Thirties section.

In 1958 much of the area at the bottom of Spring Hill and Michaelgate was demolished and eventually rebuilt. (RI-3413)

Maud's Hill Terrace was one of the terraces of houses which disappeared in the slum-clearance scheme. (RI-3413)

Houses at the bottom of Spring Hill which made way for modern properties. (RI-3413)

With the building of Pelham Bridge, a new road, for buses, was constructed, linking Melville Street and Oxford Street. On the left, Oxford House, changed from a school to an hotel, eventually being incorporated into the Grand Hotel. (RI-3821)

Houses in Napoleon Place, between Melville Street and Oxford Street, were demolished to make way for a new link road, in 1955, as part of the Pelham Bridge scheme. (RI-1173)

Lincoln's new telephone exchange was taking shape in 1956, at the corner of St Rumbold's Street and Broadgate. The old exchange was over the Head Post Office, in Guildhall Street. (RI-3849)

All of these properties in Melville Street were eventually demolished to make way for Pelham Bridge. These scenes in 1955 were taken at a time when many of the employees of Ruston and Hornsby's factory used cycles to get to and from work. (RI-3716)

Some of the old buildings to the south of the River Witham which were swept away by re-development of the area. This picture was taken in 1955. Today, you would see the bus station and car park. (RI-3860)

The old Green Dragon public house was being demolished in 1956 when this picture was taken. The 14th century merchant's house was restored and became the new Green Dragon. (RI-3972)

Hartsholme Hall was the former home of Lord and Lady Liverpool and was used in World War Two by the Airborne Division. It was demolished in 1964, leaving only the stable block, still in use as a visitor centre for Hartsholme Country Park. (RI-3967)

St Peter at Arches Church was demolished in 1933 and some of the stonework rebuilt into a new church on the St Giles Estate. The old Butter Market, at the back, remained until 1937, when a new market hall was built in Sincil Street. (RI-1933)

Old cottages in Hungate made way for a new school, St Martin's Junior Girls' and Infants. Beyond is Spring Hill Girls School. (RI -120)

Thornbridge was widened in 1939 with the increase in road traffic being too much for the old bridge. (RI-169)

Whilst work was under way widening the road at Thornbridge, a temporary footbridge was provided for pedestrians. In the background is the Old Green Dragon public house. (RI-207)

A cloud of dust rises as houses at the junction of Union Road and Westgate are pulled down in 1961. Nothing has been built on the site, but it has opened up a view of the castle's west gate. (RI-3715)

The Great Northern Hotel was built in 1848, near to the railway station, but in 1965, it was demolished and the scene of many of the city's social events disappeared. (RI-2518)

In the late Thirties, the Lincoln Co-operative Society's shop in Newport was rebuilt separating it from Newport Arch. (RI-144)

When Pelham Bridge opened in 1958, there was a traffic roundabout at the northern end, but it created more problems than it solved, so it was removed. Behind can be seen the Green Dragon, the Thornbridge Hotel and some of the old Waterside buildings yet to be demolished.

Properties in Broadgate, including a salesroom and pawnbrokers shop were demolished in 1960, to make way for a modern office block. (RI-2632)

In 1938, a new Drill Hall for the Territorial Army was built in Newport and is still in use today. (RI-157)

Houses in Melville Street were demolished in 1939 and the Thornbridge Hotel was built on the site. Now it too has gone, being replaced by a supermarket, shops and car park. (RI-207)

This was the level crossing on Skellingthorpe Road in 1932 with a Lincoln Corporation bus, bound for Burton Road running from the new Swanpool Estate. (RI-29)

The framework for the Smith's Crisps factory, on Newark Road, which opened in 1938. Today, the company name is Walkers and millions of packets of snack food are produced there each week. (RI-175)

Wragby Road in the Forties and a new wall is being built. Nearby stood The Quarry, a maternity home for unmarried mothers. (RI-191)

The old 15/16th century house on the corner of Castle Hill and Bailgate was restored in the Thirties. Later, it was to become a bank and is now the Tourist Information Office. (RI-57)

A murky day in March 1955, when this picture was taken in Broadgate. Almost all of the buildings in the foreground both left and right have now gone. (RI-3143)

A grim Victorian Workhouse changed to West View, in Lincoln, being used as a hospital for the elderly. In the early Sixties it was demolished and the site cleared for housing. (RI-1184)

St Andrew's Presbyterian Church under construction, in 1963. Today the church is St Andrew's United Reformed Church. (RI-4010)

The railway coaling plant, in Homes Yard, was demolished in 1965 on the same day that the Great Northern Hotel was razed to the ground. The 82ft-high structure had been around for almost 30 years and could hold 50 tons of coal, sufficient for ten locomotives. (RI-146)

The coaling plant for steam trains was built in 1937 and was to remain in use for almost 30 years. (RI-146)

In 1935, the country was celebrating the Silver Jubilee of King George V. Bailgate was one of the many streets in Lincoln which were decorated. (RI-165)

Moments of Celebration

WE ALL like the chance to celebrate, be it small family affairs, or the grander occasions when the whole nation joins in.

This section deals with some of these events and the pictures which were taken by *Echo* photographers to capture the atmosphere for all times.

In 1935, it was the Silver Jubilee of King George V and Queen Mary.

Many of Lincoln's buildings were floodlit and the streets were decked with bunting. Unfortunately, there are no pictures in the archives of celebration parties, although there must have been some taking place.

King George V died in 1936, to be succeeded by Edward the Eighth, but within ten months, he had abdicated and his brother became King George VI. The Coronation planned for Edward continued and in May 1937, King George VI and Queen Elizabeth were crowned in Westminster Abbey.

The event was marked in Lincoln with an exhibition at the Usher Gallery and once again, the streets showed the city's feelings with masses of red, white and blue decorations.

Street parties were held to mark the end of the war and the next time the city, and country, celebrated was the Coronation of Queen Elizabeth II, in 1953. Fortunately, a number of the *Echo* photographs taken at this time have survived and show the decorated buildings, parties and parade held through the streets, even though the weather was not on its best behaviour.

In 1977, there were celebrations again, this time for the Queen's Silver Jubilee and the *Echo's* team of photographers spent a very busy few days capturing the happy moments at some of the parties.

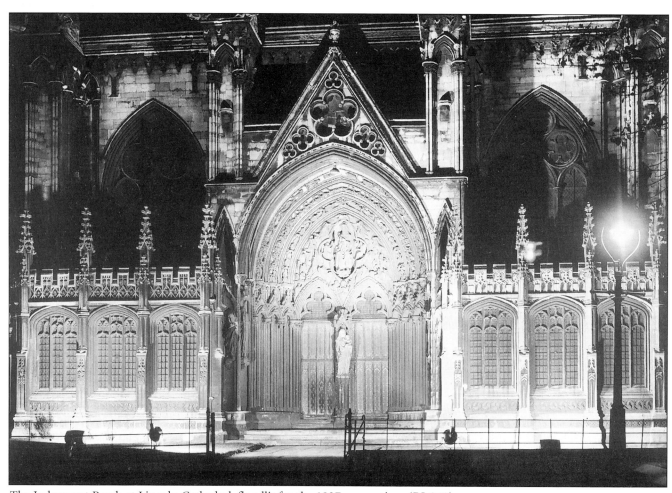

The Judgement Porch at Lincoln Cathedral, floodlit for the 1937 coronation. (RI-243)

St Mark's Church, its beauty revealed by floodlights for the 1935 Silver Jubilee celebrations. (RI-134)

The façade of The Lincoln School, on Wragby Road, in 1937. (RI-200)

Lindsey County Council offices bathed in floodlight in 1937. Today, it is the offices of the Lincolnshire County Council. (RI-201)

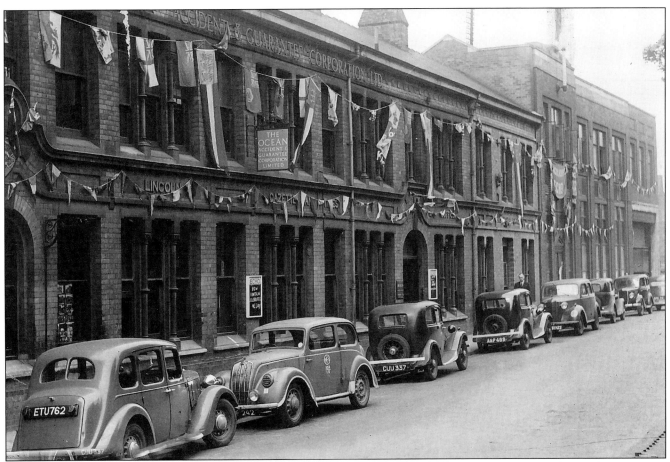

Lincolnshire Echo offices in St Benedict's Square decorated for the Coronation of King George VI in 1937. (RI-255)

1937 coronation time, and Lincoln High Street between the railway stations decorated in red, white and blue. (RI-178)

For the Coronation of King George VI in 1937, a fountain was installed in the small garden at the front of Lincoln Cornhill. (RI-202)

Residents of Rosemary Lane, Lincoln, in party mood at the end of the war in 1945.

How the *Lincolnshire Echo* brought the news of the Queen's Coronation in June 1953.

Members of the Lincoln Townswomen's' Guild presented a pageant at their 1953 Coronation Ball at the County Assembly Rooms. (RI-823)

Lincolnshire Motor Co premises in Newland in 1953. (RI-823)

Smith's Crisps factory, in Newark Road, Lincoln, was relatively new at the time of the 1953 coronation. (RI-823)

One of Lincoln Corporation's buses was especially painted for the 1953 coronation.

Silver Street and the old Corporation Offices decked out for celebrations in 1953. (RI-823)

Lincoln Cathedral, floodlit in 1953 and a ghostly figure admiring the view – but don't worry – it's the effect of the time exposure needed to make the picture. (RI-821)

They were putting up the bunting on Monks Road for the coronation in 1953, when this picture was taken, which also shows the Bull's Head public house, which was demolished in 1959. (RI-823)

Marks's and Spencer store in the High Street decorated for the 1953 coronation. (RI-823)

Residents of Hainton Road at their coronation party in 1953. (RI-823)

The north side of
Lincoln Stonebow,
not often seen in
photographs,
decorated in 1953.
(RI-823)

Lucy Tower Street in Lincoln may well have been only a small street, but it had enough residents to hold a party for the 1953 coronation. (RI-823)

Mayor of Lincoln in 1953, Councillor Ernest Coombes, presents a silver spoon to baby Kenneth Roland Gibbons, of Westwick Drive, who was born on Coronation Day (2 June). (RI-823)

The United States Air Force contingent float in the 1953 parade from the West to South Commons. (RI-823)

Ruston and Hornsby won a first prize in the Coronation Parade. (RI-823)

Judging by the look of the Lincoln Sea Cadets, at the front of this float, it was very cold for the coronation in 1953. (RI-823)

An 'Emmett' like train as a float was the choice of the Lincoln Chamber of Commerce in the 1953 Coronation Parade – and it won them a third prize. (RI-823)

Large portraits of the Queen and Duke of Edinburgh were designed by students of the Lincoln School of Art, for the 1977 Silver Jubilee. (77-088-7)

A mock battle in progress at Sanders Close jubilee party. (77-142-16)

Youngsters in fancy dress at Astwick Road's jubilee celebrations. (77-112-9)

Mayor of Lincoln, Councillor Jim Sullivan, cuts the cake at Vernon Street's party. (77-121-29)

Pupils of St Joseph's Convent School taking part in their jubilee procession. (77-077-7)

Waiting for the cake to be cut at Sidlaw Grove's Silver Jubilee party. (77-147-6)

Bottles of 'bubbly' for residents of Risby Green, at their jubilee celebrations. (77-132-4)

Judging the fancy dress at Grey Street, jubilee party are Councillor Cecil Robinson and Mrs Doreen Robinson. (77-133-6)

Pupils of Bishop King' School at their celebration for the Silver Jubilee. (77-104-7)

There was a large cake to be enjoyed by residents of Maple Street at their party in 1977. (77-144A-12)

Members of St Faiths Forget-me-not Club with some very patriotic pinnies at their party. (77-085-19)

It was thumbs-up from the youngsters in Linton Street and Ripon Street when they were asked what they thought about their jubilee party. (77-146-19)

Entertainment for the youngsters at Bell Grove, jubilee party. (77-141-17)

Fancy hats was the competition at Derby Street's party. (77-128-31)

Residents of Helsby Road and Syston Grove took no chances with the weather for their party – they held it in a tent. (77-140-36)

There was a donkey and fancy hats at this party held on Hykeham Road. (77-117-13)

Children in fancy dress at the party held by residents of Parker Avenue. (77-144-7)

Souvenir mugs for the Silver Jubilee were provided for children by St Peter at Gowts and St Andrew's Mother's Union and handed out by the vicar of St Peter's, Revd David Bates. (77-690-5)

Residents of Constable Close at their jubilee party. (77-143-32)

Lighting the Lincoln Silver Jubilee Beacon, at Birchwood, in 1977. A chain of beacons was lit all around the country. (77-135-2)

Some of the crowd who watched the lighting of the Lincoln beacon. (77-135-7)

The Fifties

THE period of the Fifties was one which was recorded by photographers in great detail. After the restrictions of the Forties, many people started taking their own photographs, films became more readily available and there were great advances in the techniques of photography.

This was the time when more and more pictures appeared in the *Lincolnshire Echo* and the special weekly picture edition, known by many simply as 'The Pic-Echo', introduced in the late Forties, continued to be published right through the decade and even into the next one.

This called for the photographers to attend many of the social events in and around Lincoln and some of these can be found in this section.

It was also the period of great change in the middle of Lincoln, with the building of Pelham Bridge to try and relieve some of the traffic problems caused by the Pelham Street and Canwick Road level crossing.

Such a big event in the city saw the first visit to Lincoln of Queen Elizabeth II, for the official opening but in this section, we have pictures of some the other venues visited by the Queen on that day in 1958.

This was also the time when Rock 'n' Roll came on to the scene and a whole host of recording stars visited Lincoln. Many of these visits can be seen in the pictures appearing the the Entertaining Moments section of this book.

Master Of The Rolls, Sir Francis Evershed (second left) during a visit to Lincoln Archives in the Exchequergate, in 1951. Also in the picture, left to right, are the Mayor, Mrs Edith Cowan, Sir Robert Pattinson, Mrs Joan Varley, Miss Williamson (Archivist) Lord Willoughby de Eresby and Mr O. B. Giles. (RI-1218)

1959 and R. M. Wright's were taking delivery of Austin cars and vans at their Newland showrooms. (RI-2932)

Mount Street School Home and School Association's Christmas party, in 1955. (RI-2040)

The Mayor of Lincoln in 1952, Councillor J. W. Giles, speaking at the laying of the foundation stone for Swallowbeck Methodist Church. On the left is Revd John Lay, who performed the ceremony. (RI-1221)

Mayor and Mayoress of Lincoln in 1954, Councillor and Mrs A. H. Briggs, joining in the fun at West View Garden Fete. West View was a home for senior citizens and was once Lincoln Workhouse. (RI-1211)

Lincolnshire Constabulary on parade and lined up for inspection in May 1957. In 1974, the county and individual town police forces were amalgamated into one force. (RI-1283)

Residents of Hope Street ready for a day's outing to the coast in 1950. (RI-628)

The first diesel train to run from Lincoln Central Station, in April 1955 was en route for Cleethorpes. (RI-991)

Holidaymakers about to board a train in 1951 to take them on their trip week holiday to Skegness. (RI-924)

Sea Ranger Mary Clarke, of Lincoln, receiving her Queen's Award from the Princess Royal at a Guides' Rally in 1950. (RI-626)

Actor Jon Pertwee (later to be better known as Dr Who), tries to master an *Echo* Linotype machine under the eye of compositor Gordon Bone. (RI-2433)

Mayor of Lincoln in 1958, Councillor Leslie Priestley, delivers his Christmas message after switching on the Cathedral floodlights. At this time, the floodlighting was only in operation during the festive season. (RI-2787)

TV actress and singer Joan Turner of Bracebridge Heath, brought her baby Anne Teresa Page, to St Hugh's Church for christening in 1953. (RI-2454)

Joan Turner at Lincoln Theatre Royal in December 1953, with theatre manager Raymond Bennett, Mayor Councillor R. E. Seely (left) and City Sheriff, Mr R. E. M. Coombes. (RI-1167)

The Band of the Royal Lincolnshire Regiment playing at a concert in Lincoln Arboretum in 1958. (RI-849)

The end of an era – Mr Charles Roberts was Lincoln's last blacksmith. His 'shop' was at 1 West Parade. (RI-1128)

In 1954, the Queen and the Duke of Edinburgh spent two days in the West Riding, Durham and Northumberland. The Royal Train (headed by locomotive *Miles Beevor*) rested for the night on its journey north, at Leadenham. When it paused for just three seconds, at Lincoln, it was to take on board Charles Carter, who 'piloted' the train to Retford. (RI-910)

Charles Carter – 'pilot' of the Royal Train, from Lincoln to Retford. (RI-910)

Labour Party leader Hugh Gaitskell (centre) with local party members posing for a picture at Newport Arch. (RI-3526)

Workmen removing the old cobbled surface at the top of Lindum Road in 1950. (RI-614)

Crowds wait in the rain for the arrival of the Queen, during her visit to Lincoln Castle in 1958. (RI-786)

The Queen meets some of the crowds who gathered at Lincoln Castle in 1958. (RI-786)

A wave from the Queen, despite the rain, at Lincoln Castle, in 1958. Accompanying the Queen is the Lord Lieutenant of Lincolnshire, the Earl of Ancaster. (RI-787)

The Queen and the Duke of Edinburgh drive around Lincoln City football ground at Sincil Bank, where a dancing display by schoolchildren had to be cancelled because of the weather. (RI-787)

A familiar sight in Lincoln for many years was the vintage Rolls Royce car operated by Cullen's for weddings and special occasions. Here, in 1953, it is being used to take the Assize Judges, from the courts to the Judges' Lodgings, accompanied by a bodyguard of policemen. (RI-1970)

Blakey's Malted Oatmeal was a nationally known breakfast cereal in 1956 and had been produced in the city for many decades. No mechanised production lines here – everything was hand packed. (RI-3622)

In 1959, there was a gent's toilet near St Marks level crossing until a goods trains was shunted into it. (RI-3700)

Checking that no one was using the toilet demolished when a goods train backed into it. (RI-3700)

It was not uncommon for swans to be seen in the streets of Lincoln, having wandered from the Brayford Pool, but just how did this bird manage to land on the Guildhall roof in 1956? (RI-3713)

Lincoln City footballers receiving polio jabs as a precaution during an outbreak of Poliomyelitis in 1959. (RI-3406)

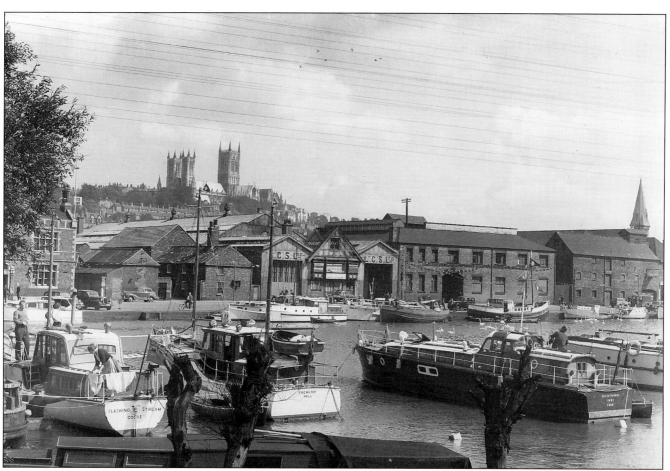

Almost all of the buildings in this 1956 picture of Brayford Wharf North have now been demolished. (RI-3816)

Boats arriving for the Boat Rally on Lincoln Brayford in 1956. In the background in the old Gas Distribution Centre. (RI-3836)

Boats preparing for the 1956 Rally, on the Brayford Pool. (RI-3816)

This picture was taken from the roof of the old *Echo* building, in St Benedict Square, in 1956. The old Brayford Head bridge can be seen, but nearly all of the buildings around the pool have now disappeared, except for the Royal William IV public house. (RI-3836)

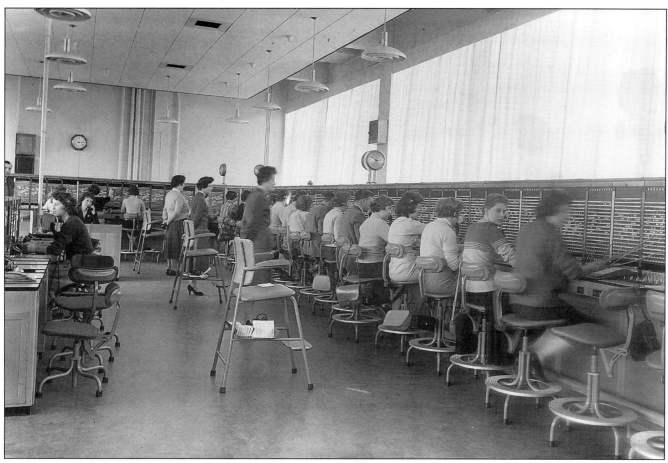

Number please! Telephonists at the switchboards of the new telephone exchange, in St Rumbold Street, which opened in 1959. (RI-3898)

National Milk Girl Zoe Newton visited Lincoln in 1957 and went appropriately to the Spotted Cow Milk Bar. (RI-2638)

Lady Cracroft-Amcotts opened the Lincoln YMCA. Ladies Auxiliary Bazaar, in October 1957. (RI-1213)

Unfortunately, there is no example of a Lincoln tram in preservation. Several of the first horse-drawn trams, which went out of service in 1905 were pressed into use as summer-houses in gardens and this one, photographed in 1953, could be seen in a garden at Waddington. (RI-2377)

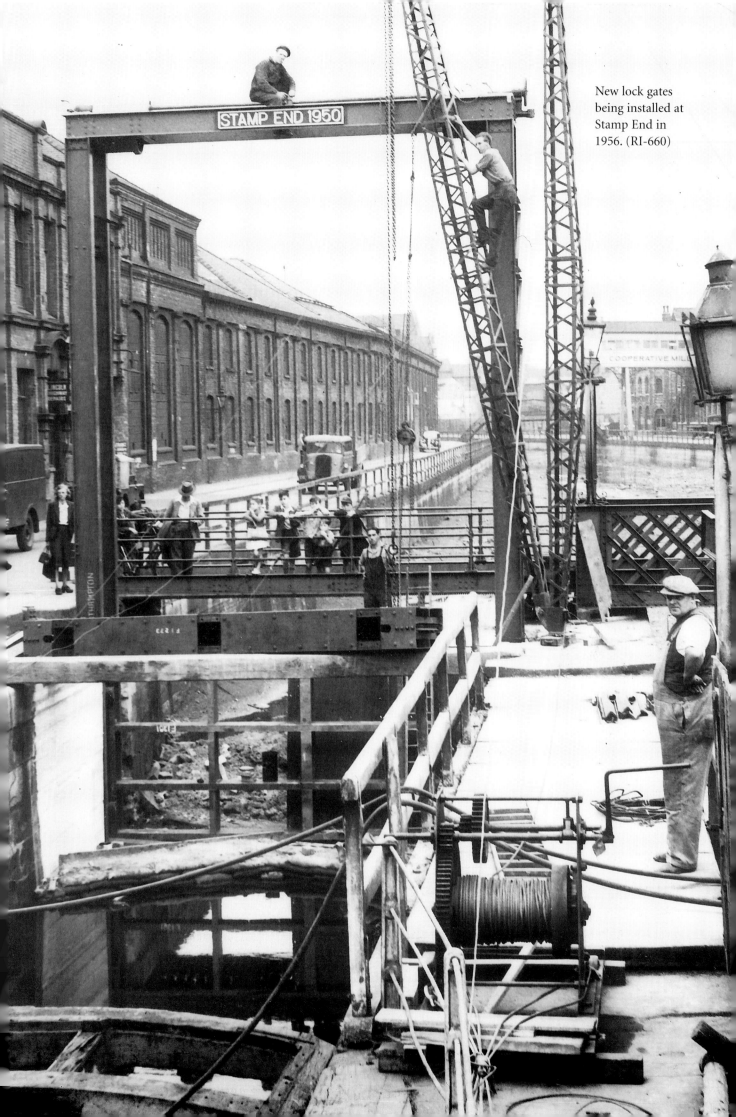

New lock gates being installed at Stamp End in 1956. (RI-660)

Workmen pause for a break as they install the lock gates in the River Witham. (RI-660)

The new Bishop of Lincoln in 1956, Rt Revd Kenneth Riches, at his enthronement. On the left is Rt Revd Maurice Harland, who was Dean of Lincoln. (RI-1349)

Mayor of Lincoln in March 1956, Councillor W. J. Bell receives a silver model of the first tank made in Lincoln, left is Mr C. V. Armitage, managing director of William Foster & Co and right is Mr William Rigsley, director of Foster's. (RI-1480)

To beat a local bus strike, in 1957, A. V. Roe used a 'Queen Mary' aircraft transporter to ferry their workers to and from the factory at Bracebridge Heath to Lincoln City centre. It was standing room only, but there was some shelter in case of rain. (RI-905)

Passengers could do nothing but wait patiently when bus crews held a stoppage over the proposal to run 'one-man' buses in 1956. (RI-2193)

Lincolnshire Road Car buses parked off St Mark's Street, in 1956, before a bus station was built a few years later. (RI-2193)

An ambulance on its way to a call in 1954, outside the old ambulance station in Melville Street. (RI-1977)

Trouble at the top of Broadgate when a water main burst in 1956, causing a large section of the road surface to crack. (RI-3170)

Pupils of Monks Road School, posing for a photograph during a 'Mind that Child' road safety campaign in 1956. (RI-3731)

It seems impossible, but motor cycle grass track racing was held on land adjacent to the Ropewalk in the Fifties. (RI-1902)

Spectators watch as running repairs are carried out during a grass track meeting at the Ropewalk. (RI-1902)

A fanfare of trumpets for the re-opening of the Regal Cinema in 1957. With the Mayor of Lincoln Councillor Mrs G. Murfin, is the cinema manger, Bill Dodds. Blowing the fanfare are the High Sheriff of Lincolnshire's trumpeters, Clem Thornton (left) and Geoff Moralee, who is still playing the fanfares more that 40 years later. (RI-1222)

Once a year. The Sincil Drain, in Lincoln, had to be cleared of weeds and plants. This work is being carried out in 1957. (RI-1034)

Councillor Alan Briggs (left of centre) chairman of the Lincoln Theatre Association, and John Hale, Lincoln Theatre Manager in 1955, when it was announced that the association had bought the theatre on behalf of the people of Lincoln. (RI-2314)

The audience show their appreciation of the announcement about the theatre's safety. (RI-2314)

Oops! This car ended up in the River Witham in 1952, having run down the very appropriately named Water Lane. (RI-794)

A well-known figure in Lincoln in the Fifties was Mr J. R. Halkes, seen here cycling along Clasketgate in October 1959 on his 90th birthday. (RI-2802)

The Princess Royal attended the Lincoln YMCA Building Fund Appeal in 1959 to receive donations of £20,000 for the appeal. In this picture, the Mayor, Alderman Fred Todd, introduces the Princess Royal to Lt Col. and Mrs H. Riggall. (RI-3959)

1953, and a parade of elephants in Lincoln High Street, moving the animals from Lincoln Central Station to Chipperfields Circus on the South Common. (RI-1861)

Marina Roper was crowned as Miss Court for the second year running in 1956. The Court School of Dancing was a popular dance venue in Lincoln and was situated in Park Street. (RI-3946)

Lincoln's MP in 1954, Geoffrey de Freitas, lays the foundation stone for St Swithin's Church Hall, built on the site of the school which was bombed during World War Two. (RI-2690)

Crowds watching the stone laying ceremony for St Swithin's Church Hall. Today, the hall is named Croft Street Community Centre. (RI-2690)

Lincolnshire's first Fox Terrier show, in 1951, attended an entry of 60 dogs. (RI-674)

Big Chief Eagle Eye rides through Lincoln on a publicity stunt for Chipperfields Circus in 1957. (RI-2145)

Perhaps this was the only time that an 'Indian Chief' rode on horseback through Lincoln stonebow. (RI-2145)

In 1954, the cinema near the River Witham was still called the Savoy. It was springtime when this picture was taken, with blossom on the trees. (RI-3904)

An unusual view under High Bridge in July 1950, with no water, but a 'railway line' for trucks carrying materials used in repair work. (RI-663)

Work was almost complete when this picture was taken in September 1950. Looking eastwards the boat *Girl Pat* is propped up and beyond can be seen the grain hoist on Doughty's Mill. (RI-620)

Workmen take a breather as they near completion of the work under High Bridge, in 1950. (RI-620)

Looking west from under High Bridge, in April 1950. The old buildings on the left and in the far distance have now gone. (RI-466)

The start of the 1952 Lincolnshire Handicap, on the Carholme, Lincoln. (RI-1250)

Anglers boarding a train at Lincoln Central Station, in 1956, to take them to the All England Angling Championships, at Kirstead, on the River Witham. (RI-3803)

Well-known presenter of *Twenty Questions* and *This is Your Life* on television, Eamon Andrews visited Lincoln Races in 1953 and met some of the local constabulary. (RI-2950)

An old Leyland Lion bus, in 1959, which used to run over routes in the city, at Young's Body Works. It has now been restored by members of the Lincolnshire Vintage Vehicle Society. (RI-2901)

A Ruston and Hornsby gas turbine mobile power station crosses the old St Mark's level crossing on route in 1959 from the Lincoln factory to a destination in Russia. (RI-2155)

Staff of Mawer and Collinghams line up for a picture before their outing to Skegness in 1957. The camera case on the right of the picture is a clue that it was taken by *Echo* photographer Mike Hollist. He regularly left his case in the picture, until at a meeting of foxhounds, one did something quite unmentionable in it. (RI-1152)

Tom Brown was a well known and respected headmaster of Bracebridge Junior School, who retired in July 1955. He is seen here with Mrs Brown receiving gifts from pupils, watched by the Mayor and Mayoress of Lincoln, Councillor and Mrs W. J. Bell, City Sheriff and his lady, Mr and Mrs L. R. Grantham and Director of Education Mr Arthur Sutcliffe. (RI-2296)

An early morning scene at Lincoln Market, with market traders unloading produce for their stalls. (59-380K)

Preparing for a busy day in 1959 at Lincoln Market. Well-known Lincoln fishmonger Bill Emery is setting up his stall. (59- 380K)

Earl Atlee, Britain's post-war Prime Minister, with Geoffrey de Freitas, Lincoln's MP, at Eastgate Court Hotel, in 1959. (RI-2687)

Road traffic was held up for 1 hour when this 4.7 inch twin gun was removed from Robey's factory on Canwick Road in 1958. The Naval gun was one of three being re-conditioned at the factory before being taken to Hull. (RI-3493)

Lincoln's last Corporation horses were retired in 1955 and left by train for Carlisle and a horses' rest home. Charles Savidge (Corporation Horse Keeper), is on the right with 17-year-old Monty, followed by Walter Rose, with Traveller. (RI-3886)

Demolition work had already started in 1956, on the Melville Street area of the city, to make way for Pelham Bridge. Some of the area was being used by the Lincolnshire Road Car bus company. In the distance can be seen St Andrew's Church, which was demolished in 1970. (RI-3812)

Entertaining Moments

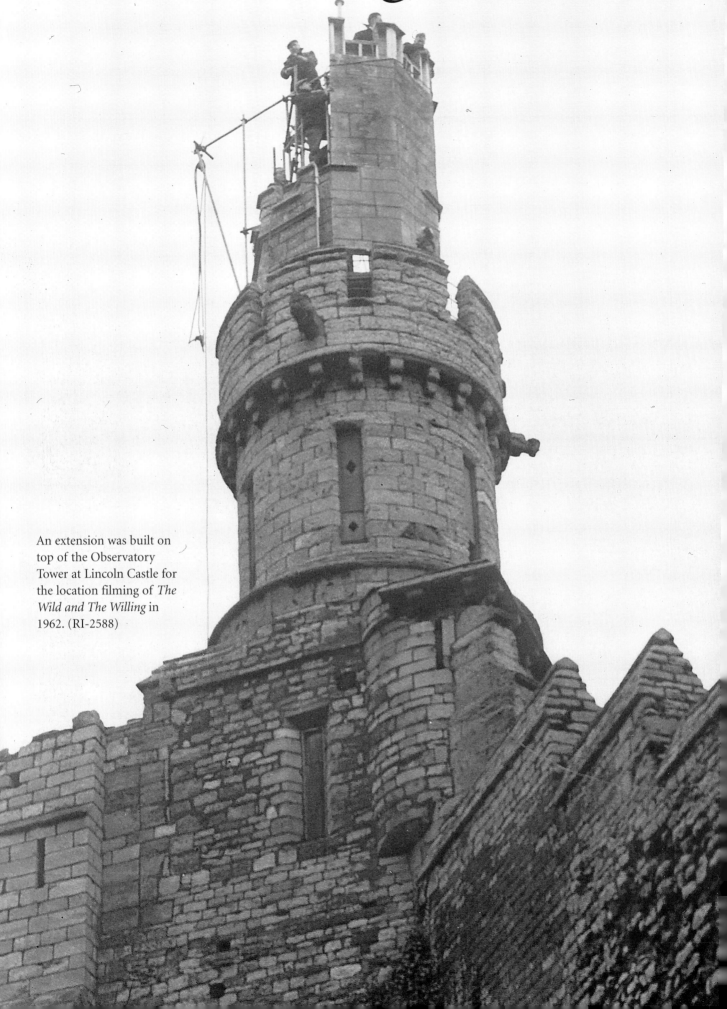

An extension was built on top of the Observatory Tower at Lincoln Castle for the location filming of *The Wild and The Willing* in 1962. (RI-2588)

THE Rock 'n' Roll years covers not one decade, but two, although many will say that it lasted even longer.

In Lincoln, the main venue for visiting recording stars was the Savoy Cinema, to be renamed halfway through the period as the ABC. It was later still to become the Cannon Cinema.

Top names appeared once a month, usually, and several of them made return visits. Announcements that they were to appear would bring queues of fans, many willing to wait all night if necessary, to get tickets for the shows, usually two in one evening.

The Drill Hall, in Broadgate, was another venue for shows.

This section of *Moments in Time* pictures some, though not all of the stars who visited Lincoln. The pictures chosen have been those which showed them with some of their lucky fans. Other pictures show the stars at the local record shop, signing autographs and making visits to a Lincoln factory.

It was also in this period that, for a few weeks, Lincoln was transformed into 'Kilminster', a red-brick university town, for the purpose of shooting location scenes for the Rank Organisation film, *The Wild and The Willing*. Amongst the cast were future stars John Hurt, Johnny Briggs and Ian McShane.

Some of the cast of the film in the grounds of Lincoln Castle. (RI-2451)

Ian McShane and Samantha Eggar talk technicalities during filming at Boultham Moor School, now Ancaster High School. (RI-2449)

The inside of the court building at the castle became the university building during the filming. (RI-2451)

The Rattlers were winners of the Lincolnshire final of the Daily Sketch Skiffle contest in 1958. (RI-3550)

Jimmy Clitheroe (centre) and Al Read (fifth from left), with some of the guests at a stage show at the ABC Lincoln in 1962. (RI-2459)

Brian Hyland signs autographs and meets his fans at the ABC Lincoln, in 1963. (RI-2440)

Eric and Ernie (Morcambe and Wise) appeared at the Savoy Cinema in 1958, before they became favourites on television. (RI-3825)

Charlie Drake made the organisers of the County Ball laugh at the dinner held before the ball in 1960. (RI-3920)

Billy Fury serenades some lucky fans between shows, at the ABC in 1962. (RI-2442)

The Avengers were one of the groups on the beat scene, playing here at the County Assembly Rooms in 1964. (RI-3384)

A youthful Bill Maynard (right) and the Beverley Sisters meet members of Lincoln Civic Party in 1958. (RI-2310)

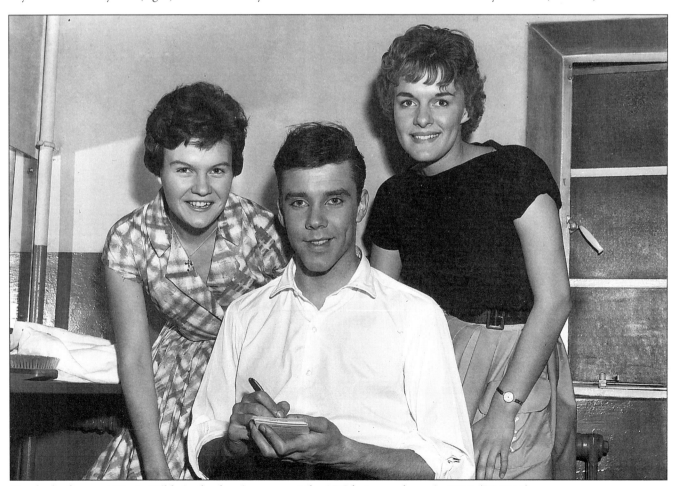

Two lucky fans met Marty Wilde in the dressing room at the ABC between shows in 1959. (RI-2813)

Waddington All Stars group put in a lunchtime appearance at Smith's Crisps canteen to entertain workers during their lunch break. (RI-3485)

A 'Softly Softly' approach by singer Ruby Murray, signing autographs for fans during a visit to Lincoln in 1956. (RI-3546)

Ronnie Hilton met some of his fans and signed autographs during his time in Lincoln in 1956. (RI-3826)

The stage door area would always attract a crowd of autograph hunters and it was no exception in 1959 when Marty Wilde was appearing at the ABC. (RI-3813)

Joan Regan signs autographs at the stage door of the Savoy Cinema, in 1958, when she appeared on the same show as Morcambe and Wise. (RI-3825)

Joan Regan pleased her fans with photographs and autographs in 1956. (RI-2308)

Records cost a bit more that *Half a Sixpence* when Tommy Steel visited in 1958. (RI-2426)

Comedian Tony Hancock raised quite a few smiles when he appeared at the ABC Lincoln, in 1958. (RI-3823)

Comedian Tommy Trinder ("You Lucky People") receives toys for the Mayor's Appeal, in 1955, from Lincoln City footballers. (RI-3381)

Funny man Joe Baker (second left) and singer David Whitfield (second right) enjoying a 'cuppa' during their visit to Lincoln in 1957. (RI-1164)

Trumpeter Eddie Calvert visited Spouge's record shop in 1956 to sign autographs for fans. (RI-3484)

The 'Peter Pan' of the pop world, Cliff Richard, pleases his fans in 1959. (RI-2889)

Fans pose with Cliff Richard on his second visit to Lincoln in 1963. (RI-2311)

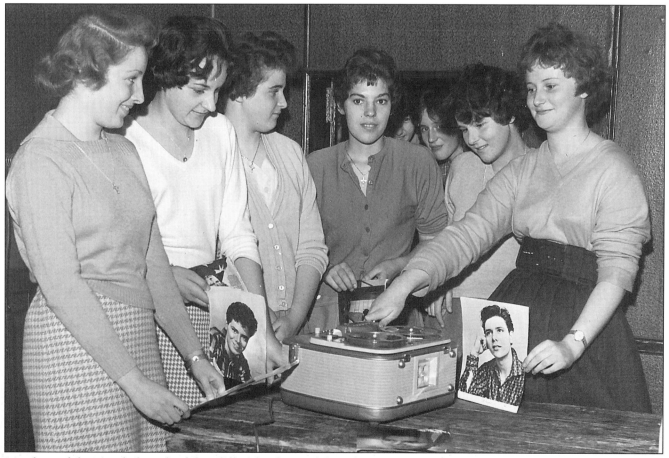

Members of the Lincoln branch of the Cliff Richard Fan Club at their party in 1959. It doesn't take too much imagination to guess what music was playing! (RI-3594)

Joan Regan poses with staff at C. R. Spouge's record shop in 1956. (RI-2308)

The Casuals, whose record *Jesamine* reached No 2 in the charts, visited the *Echo* offices in 1965 and saw how the paper was made up. (RI-3923)

There was a long wait queuing for tickets at the ABC in March 1962, when Billy Fury was on the bill. (RI-3916)

Paul Anka and Lorrea Desmond appeared at the ABC Lincoln in 1958 and met management from the theatre. (RI-1818)

Brian Hyland's hit record was *Sealed with a Kiss* when he visited Lincoln in 1963 and met some of his fans. (RI-2440)

Helen Shapiro made more than one visit to Lincoln and in 1962 met some fans in her dressing room. (RI-2442)

Anthony Newley joined the production line at Smith's Crisps when he toured the factory in 1960. (RI-3595)

Pop star Anthony Newley visited Lincoln Guildhall in 1960 and was shown the Civic Insignia by the mayor, Alderman Fred Todd. (RI-3948)

The Squires were one of the local groups of the beat scene in 1966. (RI-2952)

Al Read, radio and stage comedian meets Deslie and Pamela Renton of Lincoln, in 1959. (RI-2919)

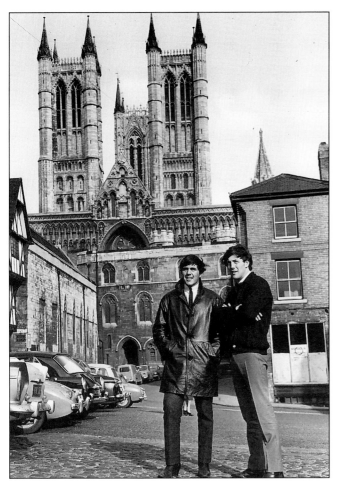

Dave Clarke (left) and drummer Mike Smith, from the Dave Clarke Five, take a look around historic Lincoln, in 1964. (RI-2434) and (right) Dave Clarke appears to be 'Glad all over' as he poses with Mike Smith, for a photograph on Steep Hill, Lincoln, in 1964. (RI-2434)

The Hollies pop group took in the Lincoln scene and posed for a picture on Waterside in 1964. (RI-2434)

Jess Conrad & Matt Munro at ABC Theatre Lincoln in April 1961. (RI-3266A)

'Arch-Goon' Harry Secombe looks rather bemused as he samples the food at the fete at Swallowbeck – could it be something to do with the sign at the back? (RI-2448)

Time for Harry Secombe to sign autographs during his visit to the fete at Swallowbeck in 1962. (RI-2448)

The Sixties

THIS was a decade which saw lots of changes in the city.

Lincoln Co-operative Society built a new store twice, only to see disastrous fires destroy both.

Demolition of property started in the Fifties and continued in the Sixties ready for the building of Wigford Way, to relieve the problems of Brayford Head bridge.

It was also a time which saw many famous names visit Lincoln, including famous politicians as well as radio and television personalities.

And it saw the end of steam trains on the railways, with the last official steam locomotive travelling through Lincoln on its way for preservation.

Many pop stars came to Lincoln at this time, and their visits have been dealt with in the section Entertaining Moments.

Circus elephants on parade crossing the railway lines in the High Street in 1961. (RI-3376)

The Lindum Players, a well known amateur theatrical group found themselves in front of a movie camera in 1963. Their plays were performed at The Little Theatre, Stanley Street. (RI-4085)

A tricky job for the crew of this lorry carrying a wide load along Monks Road in the Sixties.

Marjorie Rhodes, Liz Fraser and the Boulting brothers, John and Roy, pictured in March 1967, at St Mark's Station, Lincoln, on their way to open a new cinema in Grimsby. (RI-4038)

The Duchess of Gloucester visited the Lincoln Women's Voluntary Service in 1965 and went to both Lincoln County and St George's Hospitals to see the work of Trolley Shops. Accompanying the Duchess is Dr Charles Lillicrap. (RI-3160)

Guests at the opening of Co-operative House, in Lincoln, in 1960. Centre is the society's Managing Secretary, Mr Duncan McNab. (RI-3961)

Some of the first shoppers (including local councillors) waiting for the opening of Lincoln Co-operative Society's Silvergate House in 1960. (RI-3961)

Mr J. Mansfield, opens the rebuilt Co-operative House, after a fire, in 1965. With him are Mr Stan Bett, Managing Secretary, Mrs Mansfield and the Mayor and Mayoress of Lincoln, Councillor and Mrs George Elsey. (RI-3900)

Lincoln Co-operative Society's rebuilt premises in 1965. (RI-3899B)

Ooh-La-La… Members of the County Amateur Operatic and Dramatic Society bring a touch of 'Gay Paree' to the city in 1960, at a French Evening, held at the Green Room Club. (RI-1816)

Canon Victor Dalby was installed as Rector of Boultham in 1964. Left to right in this group are Mr L. R. W. Thrake (churchwarden), Ven A. C. Smith (Archdeacon of Lincoln), Rt. Revd Kenneth Riches (Bishop of Lincoln), Revd Colin Evans, Canon Dalby and Mr J. D. Dishman (churchwarden). (RI-1224)

Sir Charles Tennyson (left) with Brian Spiby, administrator of Lincoln Theatre Royal in 1965. Sir Charles was attending a performance of *Becket*, written by Alfred Lord Tennyson and adapted by himself. (RI-4040)

Chris Chattaway was one of the athletes who helped Roger Bannister break the four-minute mile, in May 1954. Seven years later, he visited Lincoln, calling at the Guinness Brewery's office. (RI-4207)

Assize Court officials with Judges, Mr Justice Ashworth and Mr Justice Finnemore, at Lincoln Castle in 1960. (RI-2981)

A British Waterways floating crane in use to assist with repairs to the footpath at the Glory Hole in 1964. (RI-4097)

It's not recorded if anybody cried over this load of milk bottles, which spilled from a lorry in 1965 outside the Grand Hotel. (RI-3995)

Lincoln Arboretum was opened in 1872 and has remained a popular spot ever since. This charming picture shows families using one of the many paths and in the background is All Saint's Church, on Monks Road. (RI-4272)

Work in progress on the preparations for a temporary footbridge over Brayford Head before Wigford Way was built. This picture, taken in 1963, shows the old swing bridge eventually replaced by Wigford Way. (RI-831)

The old Churchyard of St Swithin's Church was laid out as a garden of rest and is popular with those just wanting to rest, or office workers taking their lunch break. (RI-4272)

An overgrown site, on which the Central cinema once stood, is cleared to make way for a new office block in 1962. Beyond the site can be seen Lincoln Liberal Club and the ABC Cinema. (RI-3973)

Lincoln has three high rise blocks of flats. Shuttleworth House, at Stamp End; Jarvis House, at Hartsholme and Trent View on the Ermine Estate, under construction in this 1964 picture. (RI-4096)

The 4/6th Battalion, Royal Lincolnshire Regiment (TA), beating the retreat at a farewell parade for their Commanding Officer, Lt.Col G. M. Sanders, on his promotion to Colonel. (464/5)

Members of the Women's Institute leaving Lincoln in 1965 to go to Buckingham Palace. (RI-3979)

Members of British Rail Male Voice Choir leaving Lincoln Central Station, in 1961, to sing at a concert in London. (RI-4239)

A mobile crane in use to help workmen reach the chimney pots on the Treaty of Commerce public house in 1965. The other business premises, left to right, are, the Lion Hotel, Anna (Lincoln) Ltd., Shoefayre and the Lido Café. (822-128Y)

Singer Pat Parnell entertaining an audience at Moor Lodge Hotel, Branston, for 'an evening with Dennis Woodin', well known local band leader. (RI-2457)

The Mayor of Lincoln, Ald Fred Todd, inspects members of the Royal Lincolnshire Regiment in May 1960, on their farewell parade. (RI-4233)

Members of the Royal Lincolnshire Regiment on their farewell parade. (RI-4233)

One that went a bit too far was this lorry outside the Lincoln Co-operative Society's mill, on Waterside North, with its front overhanging the river, in July 1961. (RI-3991)

A recreation hall was built in 1960, for the use of nurses at Lincoln County Hospital. (RI-3896)

Lots of happy faces at the opening of Lincoln City Supporters Club, in 1964, at Sincil Bank. (RI-4290)

They had something to sing about in 1964, when Lincoln City Supporters Club opened. (RI-4290)

In August 1968, British Rail ran its last steam train and after the run, the locomotive 70013, *Oliver Cromwell* passed through Lincoln on its way to preservation in Norfolk. (G 441)

Norman Rossington, captain of the TV Entertainers football team, meets the crowd at a charity match held at Sincil Bank, in 1964, for the Western Avenue Swimming Pool Fund. (RI-1993)

There was a slight hold up to traffic in October 1956 when this excavator left Ruston-Bucyrus factory. (RI-3780)

Staff of British Home Stores in 1960 on an outing to Leicester. (RI-3884)

A very young looking Patrick Moore (second right) presenter of the television programme *The Sky at Night*, with members of the Lincoln Astronomical Society in 1961. Left to right are Peter Hammerton, Godfrey Holmes and Dr P. G. Bourne. (RI-2744)

MP for Liverpool Exchange in 1960, Bessie Braddock, speaking at a meeting of the Lincoln Labour Party Womens' Section. (RI-3592)

Members of the Lincolnshire Vintage Vehicle Society, at the Corporation Transport garage, in 1962 before visiting Ruston and Hornsby and then the site of their new museum at Whisby Road. (RI-1473)

Nationally known gardening expert Percy Thrower (right) at a gardeners' question time in Lincoln, in 1964. Also in the group are Percy Thrower's partner in the radio programme *Gardening Club*, John Warren (left), lecturer in horticulture at Riseholme Farm Institute; Wilf Lawson, from J. W. Lawson – local nurseryman and Stuart Adams, Assistant Parks Superintendent for Lincoln. (RI-2317)

The audience at the *Gardeners Question Time* show in Lincoln. (RI-2317)

Mayor of Lincoln in 1963, Councillor Mrs Hannah Kerry, cuts the cake at the Lincoln Theatre Company's eighth birthday party. (RI-1478)

A cloud of dust rises as buildings fall in Lincoln High Street in the late Sixties to make way for Wigford Way.

When students at the Lincoln School of Art held a fashion show in 1965, the fact that Lincoln didn't have an ice rink was no deterrent for one student, who designed a skating dress and carried ice skates. Lincoln still doesn't have an ice rink! (RI-3283)

Classical lines being modelled by students of the Lincoln School of Art at their fashion show in 1965. (RI-3283)

A variety of outfits designed and worn by Lincoln School of
Art Students at the fashion show in 1965. (RI-3283)

Lincoln MP Geoffrey De Freitas, looks at the Ruston Car,
returned to the city for restoration in 1963 with Mr C. T.
Alderson, one of the directors of the company. (RI-2918)

A popular event on the Lincoln dance calendar was the annual Castle Ballroom School of Dancing's ball, usually attended by Victor Silvester and his Orchestra. The bandleader (third from left) is seen here with the ballrooms proprietors and instructors Laurence (left) and Audrey Highton (third from right). (RI-2437)

Echo photographers Ken James, Stan Wing and Peter Washbourn look at some of their photographs on display at an exhibition held at the Theatre Royal in 1965. (RI-2462)

Some of the guests at the opening of the *Echo* photograph exhibition. (RI-2462)

Discussing the merits of *Echo* photographs at the exhibition, are left to right, Kenneth Gribble (principal of Lincoln School of Art), Alderman John Spence, Peter Wright and *Echo* editor Frank Shelton. (RI-2462)

It caused a bit of a sensation when this topless dress appeared in the window of Eve Brown's dress shop on the High Bridge, in 1964. However, no one saw anybody wearing one around Lincoln. (RI-2878)

A familiar sight in the west end of Lincoln for many years, has been horses and riders from the Park Riding School going from the stables in Newland Street West to the West Common, for exercise. They are pictured here in 1966 on Hewson Road. (RI-2899)

A dangerous situation at the bottom of Lindum Road, in 1967, when a fuel tanker crashed and overturned. (RI-2921)

The great star of silent movies Charlie Chaplin, with his wife Oohna, visited Lincoln Cathedral in 1964, picture here with the Dean, the Rt Revd Colin Dunlop and *Echo* chief reporter, Fred Morton. (RI-2694)

Charlie Chaplin with Oohna and Dean Colin Dunlop, in the Chapter House of Lincoln Cathedral. (RI-2694)

Moments of Our Youth

EVERYONE has memories of certain moments in their youth and these pictures will jog the memories of those who appear in them, now no longer so youthful and many with children of their own.

The pictures in this section cover a whole variety of youthful activities. Many pictures were taken by *Echo* photographers at school events, both indoors and out and some of the religious processions which used to take place are included.

A regular entertainment for children was the Saturday morning cinema clubs, before the days of all-day television and pictures of these can be seen.

There are also memories of the old Boultham Baths, where the water was always cold, but it didn't matter to the younger generation, they still enjoyed their swim. And Brayford Pool, back in the middle of the century attracted both young anglers and swimmers.

Skipper Ross was one Lincoln's characters, who ran pleasure trips along the Fossdyke aboard the *Mary Gordon* (in the background). He is seen here telling his yarns to a very interested group of schoolboys. *Mary Gordon* has now returned to Lincoln, is being restored and has been accepted on to the National Register of Historic Vessels. When restored it will be the largest electric powered boat in the country. (RI-803)

The Boys' Brigade Pyramid Display Team in action at the 1964 Lincoln Youth Show. (RI-1552)

Before the days of health clubs and fitness centres, many young ladies were members of the Lincoln Ladies' Keep Fit Association, some seen here at the 1964 Lincoln Youth Show held at Saint Peter and Saint Paul's School, Lincoln. (RI-1551)

A happy scene at the opening of Hartsholme Infants' School in June 1953. (RI-1228)

Christine Orange School of Dance pupils who won their class at the Scunthorpe Music, Drama and Dance festival in 1959. (RI-3914)

Children of members of the Lincoln and District Referees' Association at their party in 1967. (RI-2836)

End of term in summer, 1953 and sixth formers at South Park High School gather for a school leavers party in the school hall. (RI-1508)

Pupils of St Faiths Junior School, in 1957, rehearsing for their open day. (RI-2302)

Dennis Black was projectionist at the ABC Cinema, Lincoln and also Bimbo the clown, teaching road safety to local children with the help of Bertie the Beacon. (RI-3917)

Pupils of St Faiths School on an outing, in 1958, to Barton upon Humber. (RI-2291)

"I Gotta Horse" was the famous cry of Prince Monolulu, a racing tipster with a colourful head-dress. He is seen here at Lincoln Races, in March 1956, with a group of youngsters. (RI-3845)

Young pupils from St Faith's School watch as Louis Clarke makes up the *Echo* pages in 1962. (RI-3921)

Pupils from St Martin's Junior School, Lincoln, see how the news is produced during a visit to the *Lincolnshire Echo* offices. (RI-3509)

School leaving time for pupils of Oxford House School, on West Parade, Lincoln. The school was originally in Oxford Street, but had moved to new premises when this picture was taken in 1965. (RI-1803)

Far Newland Congregation Church Sunday School members at their party in 1963. (RI-1804)

Some were interested in the music, while others were more interested in the horse when William Tinmore, of Norwich, brought his barrel organ to Lincoln. (RI-3833)

The Corpus Christi procession from St Hugh's Church to St Joseph's Convent involved those taking part in a long climb up Lindum Road. These pictures were taken in 1954. (RI-1243)

Young people taking part in the 1957 Diocesan Youth Pilgrimage arrive at Lincoln Cathedral. (RI-1279)

Time for fun at Boultham Baths in the summer holidays of 1960. (RI-3932)

Enjoying their summer holiday with a visit to Boultham Baths in August 1960. (RI-3952)

Some of the competitors at the Age Group Swimming Gala, at Wickham Baths, in 1967. (RI-1068)

Starting one of the races at the Age Group Swimming Gala in 1967. (RI-1068)

Competitors in the 1956 Lincoln schools' Swimming Gala at Boultham Baths. Presenting the awards was Councillor W. J. Bell, deputy mayor. (RI-3787)

Mrs Macleans Merry mascots entertained in Lincoln for many years, but with a change of youngsters, of course. In 1936 they performed *Babes in the Wood* at the County Assembly Rooms. (RI-541)

In September 1959, it was warm enough to entice youngsters to swim in Brayford – the less hardy were content with fishing. (RI-2914)

Pupils of St Peter and St Paul's School, Lincoln, in 1958, who took part in the School's second sports day. (RI-2293)

One of the events in progress at St Peter and St Paul's School Sports. (RI-2293)

The young fishermen of England – well, Lincoln, at least, hoping for a good catch in the Brayford in 1954. (RI-1942)

At least they caught something, but it is not recorded just what. (RI-1942)

Lincoln Scouts and Rovers leave Lincoln Central Station in July 1957, for the World Jamboree in Sutton Coldfield. (RI-1173)

Before the days of childrens' television, a familiar voice on the radio was that Derek McCulloch, better known as Uncle Mac, who opened the Bookworms' Club at Lincoln Central Library in 1955. His familiar 'signing off' phase was "Goodnight children, everywhere." (RI-1166)

Monks Road Baptist Church members on an outing to Sutton-on-Sea in 1962. (RI-3882)

The children were going away on their annual family holiday in 'Trip Week', 1951, when they met up with a calf which was also travelling on the train. (RI-924)

The Lincoln Salvation Army band led the 1951 Whit Sunday parade for a rally at Lincoln's Wesley Chapel. (RI-1295)

Members of local Sunday Schools walked in procession from Lincoln Central Station to the Wesley Chapel in Clasketgate for their rally in 1951. (RI-1295)

Children of Lincoln Prison Officers at their Christmas party in 1956. (RI-3311)

Mr F.A. Stuart, Lincoln's Chief Education Officer in 1964, presents the Sampey Cup, for road safety, to Mount Street Primary School. It is being received by Head Girl, Ann Atkin. (RI-4306)

St Hugh's Boys' Home seem to be having more that just a day out in 1951, as they board a bus to take them to Skegness. (RI-3238)

Youngsters having fun in the summer holidays of 1965, at Queen's Park playground. (RI-4079)

Pupils of Boultham Moor Girl's School who took part in a Nativity Play in December 1962. (RI-4293)

Taking aim at the Lincoln School Garden Party, in June 1963. (RI-1430)

Interval time, and 'lollies' on sale at an ABC minor Saturday morning film show in 1961. (RI-4039)

The City School, Lincoln, leavers in the summer of 1961 at a service in St Mark's Church, Lincoln. Centre is headmaster Mr Leslie Middleton and to his right is Cannon Ozzie Jones, school chaplain and vicar of St Marks. (RI-3981)

Some of the dancers at a Rock 'n' Roll Carnival dance held at St Michael's Church Hall on Steep Hill. in 1958. (RI-3125)

How to order photographs
from Lincoln Moments in Time

Photographs in Moments in Time all come from the *Lincolnshire Echo* archives and prints can be ordered from the Photo Sales Department at the *Echo*.

Please quote the number at the end of the caption (where printed), plus the first line of the caption and page number.

Prices (including 17.5% VAT) are:
7"x 5" (18x12.5cms) approx………£3.50 Postage…75p.

10"x 8" (25x18cms) approx………£5.50 Postage…75p.

16"x 12" (40.6x30.5cms) approx………£7.99 Postage…£1.65.

No responsibility will be accepted for damage to prints sent through the post.
Cheques should be made payable to the Lincolnshire Publishing Company.

World copyright of all *Echo* photographs shall belong to the *Lincolnshire Echo*.

Photo Sales Department
Lincolnshire Echo Group Newspapers
Brayford Wharf East
Lincoln, LN5 7AT
Tel: (01522) 804342